Group's

EMERGENCY RESPONSE
Handbooklet:

DIVORCE

Group

Loveland, Colorado

www.group.com

Group's Emergency Response Handbooklet: Divorce

Copyright © 2008 Group Publishing, Inc.

Visit our Web site: **www.group.com**

Credits

Editor: Roxanne Wieman
Project Manager: Pam Clifford
Chief Creative Officer: Joani Schultz
Art Director: Jeff Storm

Book Designer: Pamela Poll
Cover Art Designer: Jeff Storm
Print Production Artist: Stephen Tiano
Production Manager: Peggy Naylor

Unless otherwise indicated, all Scripture quotations are taken from the *Holy Bible*, New Living Translation, copyright © 1996, 2004. Used by permission of Tyndale House Publishers, Inc., Carol Stream, Illinois 60188. All rights reserved.

978-07644-3706-9
10 9 8 7 6 5 4 3 2 1   17 16 15 14 13 12 11 10 09 08
Printed in Canada.

Contents

Introduction

It's not easy going through a divorce. But it doesn't have to be lonely.

Christians should never have to face trials on their own. Those around them—their Christian brothers and sisters—should rise up and support them.

"Share each other's burdens, and in this way obey the law of Christ" (Galatians 6:2).

Although it isn't easy to go through a divorce, it's also tough being on the outside and trying to help.

You don't know what to do. You're worried about hurting their feelings or stepping on their toes or saying the exact *wrong* thing.

Of course you care—you love them! It isn't that you don't want to help—it's just that you don't know how.

Group's Emergency Response Handbooklet: Divorce will help you come alongside your friends and those in your small group who are facing tough times. From care and counseling tips, to practical ideas for your small group, to what to say and what not to say, this booklet offers insight after insight into how to care for those who are struggling with divorce.

Of course, it'd be great if you never had to pick up this booklet! But the reality is that many couples end their marriage in divorce—including your friends and the people in your small group. And they need your help.

So when someone you love is facing divorce, it's time to pick up this guide. Use the table of contents to find the specific section that gives you what you need to be successful in helping them.

In this handbooklet there is a **real life narrative**—a story from someone who's been there. You'll find a section on **care and counseling tips** that will give you practical ideas for reaching out in love. The practical ideas in the **group tips** section will help your entire small group support your hurting friends during their trial. An invaluable section on **what to say and what not to say** to your friends. This section will help you avoid the hurtful comments and use the helpful ones.

You'll also find useful boxes that offer Scripture help, guidelines for referring your friend to a professional counselor, and additional resources, such as books and Web sites, that you can use as you support your hurting friends.

Our prayer for this booklet is that it will help you help your friends during a difficult time.

Divorce

Helping Your Friend Cope
With All of Its Difficulties

with counseling insights from **TERRI S. WATSON, PSY.D.**
+ ministry tips from **JOY-ELIZABETH F. LAWRENCE**

After almost 30 years of marriage, Maria made the difficult decision to file for divorce from her husband, Kevin. Although Maria believes that marriage is for life—through the good and the bad—Kevin had a history of marital infidelity and had not changed despite several years of counseling and church discipline.

Emergency Response Handbooklet: *How did your church respond to your divorce?*

Maria: The church called a congregational meeting since Kevin was the head elder. Kevin hadn't been attending the church for a while because of what was happening between us and because he traveled, which I'd used as a handy excuse when people asked where he was. Anyway, at the meeting the pastor said, "We called this meeting because we want to tell you that Kevin is under church discipline for moral failure." He asked the congregation to pray for my kids and me and also told them to address all questions to himself rather than to my family or me.

ERH: *How did your small group and Christian friends respond?*

Maria: There were times when I needed to talk about what I was going through, and this is what taught me who my friends really were. I had one friend who was really close, but she totally backed away. Another friend would talk about anything *but* what I was going through. Everything was all "hush, hush" and under wraps, but I didn't really want that. Also, when you're a couple and you do things with other couples and then are divorced, you don't get included in couple things anymore.

I did a Bible study together with a core group of female friends (a different Bible study than mentioned earlier). Those ladies were my support group. They prayed for me diligently, and there was no way that I would have been able to walk that path and go through what I went through without them. I had seen other women go through divorce and wind up very angry, malicious, and ugly.

ERH: *How did you feel being a divorcing—and now divorced—Christian?*

Maria: Well first, there are the shame issues. That's a huge thing in Christian circles. I really had to work through that and was helped a lot by passages in Isaiah and Psalms.

Secondly, I was embarrassed. For what my husband had done, that I'd gotten myself in this situation, and that as a Christian I was going through divorce. Being divorced carries a stigma. Not that when I look at other divorced women I think of them badly, but it's hard being divorced. When you're a widow, there's definitely more sympathy. It's OK to be a widow, but you have control over whether or not you're divorced.

I was angry, too, but I was careful of how and when I expressed it. I know that unwillingness to forgive slides a person into bitterness really quickly. But it was hard. I kept thinking, "This is horrific. This is my whole life. My married life was a lie."

ERH: *Do you have advice for others regarding forgiveness in the situation of infidelity and divorce?*

Maria: Forgiveness is a two-part thing. First, forgiveness isn't about the other person, it's about yourself. You have to let go of the right to retaliate, the desire to hurt him as badly as he hurt you. It doesn't happen all at once; it's a process that comes in stages; it ebbs and flows. There are layers to it like an onion. You get through one layer; then something will happen, and you'll have to peel the next layer.

Secondly, I had to understand that forgiving him didn't make what he did OK or mean that I condoned it. In the end I didn't forgive because of him, I forgave because it was a step of help for me. I told him, "As much as I know to this point, I forgive you."

ERH: *How would you summarize your experience of divorce?*

Maria: To me, divorce is a death. It's the death of a relationship. A lot of people will quote Romans 8:28: "And we know that in all things God works for the good of those who love him, who have been called according to his purpose" (New International Version). I don't believe that the divorce was "good", but I believe that "all things" means the big picture—everything, the bad and the good, rolled into one. It means that eventually God works it for good.

WHEN TO REFER

Most individuals going through a divorce can benefit from some professional counseling at some point in the process, particularly if they have children. Don't hesitate to encourage your friend to seek professional help immediately if any of the following signs and symptoms are present.

+ References to self-destructive or suicidal thoughts or feelings

+ Isolative behavior

+ Continuous "bad-mouthing" of the ex-spouse in the presence of others, particularly the children

Offering to sit with your friend during the initial call or accompanying him or her to an appointment can ensure that your friend receives the immediate help he or she needs.

Care and Counseling Tips

THE BASICS

A divorce is a vulnerable time for a Christian, but the love of Christ, expressed through Christian community, can make all the difference. You or your small group can offer Christ's love through competent and informed Christian caring, which involves understanding the many challenges, transitions, and effects of divorce.

Practical concerns—Divorce affects dramatic changes in the person's day-to-day tasks. The person may need to secure a new place to live, take care of household tasks alone, maintain or seek employment, and manage finances.

Restructuring of relationships—The effects of divorce are felt in nearly all of the divorcing person's relationships. Extended family may offer support, but relationships with in-laws can become strained. Some couple friendships are lost because many couples feel "caught in the middle" as they try to maintain friendships with both parties.

Emotional effects—After the initial shock, divorced people often cycle through stages of anger, sadness, grief, and confusion before reaching a stage of acceptance in which they "move on" with their lives. Divorcing parents must also face the task of providing support and care for their children.

Spiritual struggles—Following divorce, feelings of disillusionment toward marriage, the Christian life, and the church often create distance from God and make it difficult to trust him. Spiritual struggles are compounded by issues such as anger toward the ex-spouse and difficulties in forgiving. Some may also feel that God did not answer prayers for marital reconciliation.

Care Tips

The good news is that social support received from others can minimize the long-term damaging effects of divorce on the heart and soul of an individual and his or her family. Caring for your friend's practical needs in a time of crisis is an important expression of Christ's love and will solidify your commitment to walk with the person through the divorce experience. The following suggestions focus on how you and your small group can help with the practical needs of your friend. (Keep in mind that it's probably best—and most appropriate—for men to reach out to men and women to women in this situation. Especially for ongoing and one-on-one care and counseling.)

+ Identify immediate needs.
When a friend discloses that he or she is going through a divorce, it's important to follow up after the group meeting to find out more about the circumstances. Don't be afraid to ask about specifics, and encourage your friend to share immediate needs (you may want to make a list). Affirm your friend's courage in sharing those needs with the group, and remind your friend that "bearing one another's burdens" is what Christian community is all about!

+ Be the "point person" in mobilizing the resources of the church.
Churches possess tremendous practical resources for a person going through a divorce. Coordinate the matching of church resources with areas of need that have been identified. Consult with your pastor to identify church members who can offer financial advice, legal counsel, child care, vocational guidance, and assistance in finding affordable housing. Offer to make the initial call to connect your friend with others who can assist in practical ways.

+ Utilize the resources of your group.

You need look no further than your small group for resources that can be a tremendous support in the day-to-day practical challenges of a divorce. Practical ways for your group to help include providing child care, going with the person to court dates and legal appointments, connecting your friend with the local community college to explore vocational options, and initiating "nights out" on a regular basis to take your friend to a movie or dinner.

+ Offer information.

Knowing what to expect when going through a divorce can reduce anxiety, provide a greater sense of control, and normalize some of the difficult emotional components. Connect your small group member with others in the church who have gone through a divorce. Provide your friend with information about a divorce support group in the community. Consider giving your friend a Christian self-help book on divorce, and offer to meet together weekly to read and discuss. Anything you can do to offer information will help your friend tremendously!

SCRIPTURE HELP

These Scriptures can help you and your friend as you work through the difficulties of divorce.

+ **Job 42:1-3**
+ **Psalm 20**
+ **Psalm 27:1-3**
+ **Ecclesiastes 3:11**
+ **Isaiah 43:2-3**

+ **Romans 15:7**
+ **2 Corinthians 1:3-5**
+ **2 Corinthians 4:7-8**
+ **Philippians 2:12-13**
+ **James 5:7-8**

Counseling Tips

Helping the divorcing person with the emotional, relational, and spiritual effects of divorce requires long-term involvement. This is a crucial ministry that can make a huge difference in the emotional and spiritual well being of the person and of his or her children. Here are some tips to help you as you counsel your friend.

+ Listen actively and nonjudgmentally.
Meet with your friend on a regular basis, and make it your goal to actively listen. Encourage the person to express fears, concerns, frustrations, and disappointments. Be empathetic and understanding. Resist the urge to "fix things" or give advice during these times—your task is simply to love! Be sensitive to the promptings of the Holy Spirit during these meetings. Be a good "sounding board" as your friend tries to negotiate the many tasks and challenges of a divorce. End your meetings together with prayer, and commit to pray specifically for your friend on a daily basis.

+ Anticipate and plan for stressful transitions.
Going through a divorce is one of the most painful and stressful experiences an adult can face. You can be a tremendous help by assisting in the anticipation and planning for the many challenges of divorce. For example, what will it be like for your friend to see his or her spouse in court or to meet the new partner at one of the children's sporting events? Talking through these scenarios, practicing the desired response through role-playing, and anticipating times when extra support is needed are ways to normalize and manage the stress of these transitions.

+ Help your friend assess his or her feelings toward the spouse.
The intense and conflicting feelings toward the divorcing spouse are a common place where people get "stuck" in the divorce process. Strong feelings

toward one's ex, if not worked through, can result in long drawn-out legal battles, damaging experiences for children, and a lifetime of bitterness. Providing your friend the opportunity to express and work through these feelings can be a huge source of support. Allow some degree of "venting" (better with you than with the children!). Discourage "black and white" thinking about the ex, such as "she's all bad" or "it's all his fault." Encourage forgiveness and "letting go."

+ Support healthy co-parenting.
When the divorcing person has children, consider the needs of the whole family. Children's adjustment to divorce is significantly better if they can maintain good relationships with both parents. Encourage co-parenting, and be supportive of visitation and custody arrangements. Discourage "spouse bashing" in the presence of children. Encourage your friend not to rely on his or her children for emotional support but develop the adult friendships available in your group. Be a friend to the children, and offer to connect them with additional sources of support.

+ Encourage your friend to have hope for the future.
With every crisis and loss come opportunities for growth, ministry, and new and healthier relationships with God and others. At the right time, encourage your friend to focus on the possibilities available to him or her, and empower your friend to trust God for his or her future.

+ Don't be afraid to pray for reconciliation.
With God's help, your friends may eventually come back together again. Don't be afraid to hope for this!

Group Tips

Feelings of isolation, loneliness, and shame often keep divorcing Christians from utilizing the resources offered by the Christian community. Know that these feelings may make your group member seek to drop out or disappear from the group during this difficult time—a time when he or she most needs that support. Encourage your group to reach out to their friend—no matter what!

+ If the couple divorcing are both involved in your small group, keep the following in mind:

It's very difficult for a small group when attempts to support reconciliation have failed and a couple chooses to pursue divorce. Feelings of failure, disappointment, and disillusionment can ensue and should be acknowledged. Group members should be discouraged from taking sides. The group can continue to promote redemption of the situation by encouraging an amicable relationship: treating one another with respect, cooperating in co-parenting, and so on. It's not likely that both members of the couple will maintain membership in the group. Consider making the decision cooperatively about who will continue to attend. Which spouse appears to need the group more? Who is at greatest risk of isolation? Who has the most responsibility for the children and may need the greatest practical assistance? Help the person leaving the group to find another place for his or her own support and spiritual growth.

+ Provide a place to belong.

Offering a place of true belonging goes a long way in combating the feelings of isolation that are part of divorce. Be explicit in your commitment as a group to walk through this difficult experience with the person. Watch out for—and discourage—judgmental or harmful comments toward your friend. Encourage your friend to commit to attend your group meetings. Pursue your friend, even if he or she withdraws. And don't let your friend sit alone in church!

+ Offer a safety net for stressful times.

Sometimes the stress of divorce hits unexpectedly, and knowing there is a safety net of caring friends makes all the difference. Provide an index card with a list of names and numbers of group members whom the person can call when in need of emotional support, child care, fellowship, or prayer.

+ Create a healthy, supportive group atmosphere.

Make sure all group members are sharing their own struggles and seeking support. As a group, commit to engage in honest acknowledgement of areas of sin and brokenness. Be accountable, confess your sins to one another, and actively promote forgiveness and reconciliation of differences. Seek to restore faith, hope, and love within your group. Remember, we can love each other only because God first loved us.

A "HEALTHY" DIVORCE

Although a divorce is rarely a welcome or positive experience in the life of a person, a "healthy" divorce is possible—one that minimizes the damage to the individuals involved, particularly if the couple has children. Recognizing the characteristics of healthy adjustment in divorce can help the small group provide competent, intentional caring as a member faces the difficult transition of divorce.

1. Both parents remain involved with children in order to provide a continued sense of "family."

2. Children are protected from the more negative impacts of divorce.

3. Both spouses are able to accept and integrate the divorce into their thinking about themselves and their future in a healthy way.

—Characteristics taken from: Carter, Betty and McGoldrick, Monica, Eds. *The Expanded Family Life Cycle: Individual, Family, and Social Perspectives,* Third Edition. Needham Heights, MA: Allyn and Bacon, 1999.

What Not to Say

Keep in mind that the worst thing a friend can do is say nothing, which only intensifies the feelings of isolation and estrangement. When it's said in the spirit of true love and caring, even saying the wrong thing with good intentions is an act of caring. Here are some specifics to keep in mind.

+ "God hates divorce."
We need to love, not judge. Regardless of our views on divorce, broken relationships happen in the church due to the presence of sin in the world. When a friend is going through a divorce, it's a time to show God's love, healing, and grace.

+ "It's not your fault."
Eventually, part of the process of healing involves recognizing, confessing and seeking forgiveness from God and the ex-spouse for one's own role in the breakdown of the marriage. Balance mercy and love with truth—don't discourage acceptance of personal responsibility.

+ "You've shared too much. I don't need to know that."
Most divorces are messy, and it's important to listen to someone when he or she needs to talk. Listen to the stories, even if it's hard for you. Besides, listening to your friend can help you assess where he or she is in the healing process, and what he or she most needs right now.

What to Say

+ "I don't know what to say."
If you don't know what to say, don't avoid speaking to the person! Just approach him or her and say, "I'm sorry about what's happening. I wish I had something to say, but I don't know what to say." Then, be open for whatever conversation comes up.

+ "Please join us."

After a divorce, many people are lonely. They miss the companionship that came with marriage. Sadly though, divorced people are often left out of social situations because they're not a pair. Don't let this happen! Invite your friend to dinner or a movie. If you're afraid he or she will be uncomfortable, *ask*.

+ "How can we help you this week?"

Do check in weekly with the person to identify specific areas of need and prayer requests, and to anticipate upcoming transitions. It's often difficult for people to initiate asking for help during times of vulnerability.

+ "We live in a broken world, and that affects every-thing—even love."

It can be a meaningful experience to acknowledge, together, that the brokenness, sinfulness, and grief we experience in this life are so far from God's ideal for us. Some people find it easy to turn to God in the midst of suffering. For others, it's a difficult task to trust in God's goodness. Life on this earth is often unfair, and many times it can feel like there is no justice in the aftermath of a divorce. Longing together for our eternal life with Christ—when there will be no more tears (Revelation 21:4)—can be a helpful reminder of the new heaven and earth in store for Christians.

RECONCILIATION

If a couple you are friends with or are in your small group is struggling in their marriage and possibly facing a divorce, try to help the couple in the reconciliation process.

✚ Encourage them to consider the small group a safe meeting place for both of them.

✚ Don't take either person's side—try to be an objective mediator.

✚ Encourage them to seek professional marriage counseling.

✚ Recommend that they try a HomeBuilders study (www.group.com) together or another course aimed at strengthening marriage.

ADDITIONAL RESOURCES

✚ Books

Burns, Bob and Whiteman, Tom. *The Fresh Start Divorce Recovery Workbook: A step-by-step program for those who are divorced or separated.* Nashville, TN: Thomas Nelson, Inc. Publishers, 1998.

Hart, Archibald D. *Helping Children Survive Divorce.* Dallas, TX: Word Publishing, 1996.

Richmond, Gary. *Successful Single Parenting.* Eugene, OR: Harvest House Publishers, 1990.

Kniskern, Joseph Warren. *When the Vow Breaks: A Survival and Recovery Guide for Christians Facing Divorce.* Broadman & Holman Publishers, 1993.

✚ Online Resources

www.divorcecare.com
www.freshstartseminars.org

GROUP'S EMERGENCY RESPONSE HANDBOOKLET SERIES

Addiction. Depression. Divorce. Financial crisis. Rebellious children. Every day people face these difficult challenges---but they don't have to go it alone. Now Group's Emergency Response booklets can equip anyone to reach out to hurting friends with love and confidence! Each topic-specific pamphlet holds powerful ways to minister to a struggling friend. Discover counseling and care tips, practical advice on what to say and not say, Scripture connections, and additional resources.

Addiction	ISBN 978-0-7644-3620-8	10-pack
Depression	ISBN 978-0-7644-3619-2	10-pack
Divorce	ISBN 978-0-7644-3621-5	10-pack
Financial Crisis	ISBN 978-0-7644-3622-2	10-pack
Rebellious Child	ISBN 978-0-7644-3623-9	10-pack
Addiction	ISBN 978-0-7644-3705-2	Single copy
Depression	ISBN 978-0-7644-3704-5	Single copy
Divorce	ISBN 978-0-7644-3706-9	Single copy
Financial Crisis	ISBN 978-0-7644-3707-6	Single copy
Rebellious Child	ISBN 978-0-7644-3708-3	Single copy

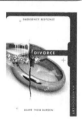